CHART HITS OF 2013-2014
FOR UKULELE

ISBN 978-1-4803-7108-8

HAL•LEONARD®
CORPORATION
7777 W. BLUEMOUND RD. P.O. BOX 13819 MILWAUKEE, WI 53213

Visit Hal Leonard Online at
www.halleonard.com

Blurred Lines

Words and Music by Pharrell Williams and Robin Thicke

1. If you can't hear what I'm try'n' to say,

if you can't read from the same page, may-be I'm go-in' deaf,

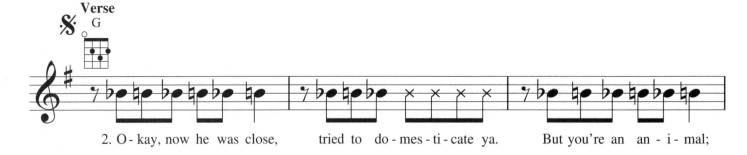

may-be I'm go-in' blind, may-be I'm out of my mind.

Verse

2. O-kay, now he was close, tried to do-mes-ti-cate ya. But you're an an-i-mal;

ba-by, it's in your na-ture. Just let me lib-er-ate ya, you don't need no pa-pers.

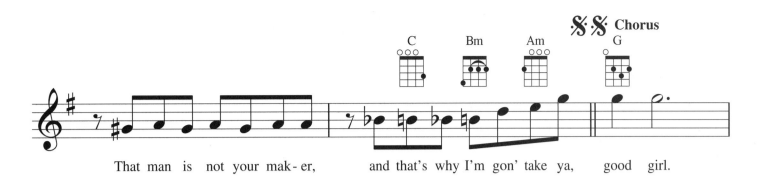

That man is not your mak-er, and that's why I'm gon' take ya, good girl.

I know you want it. I know you want it. I know you want it. You're a

good girl. Can't let it get past me. You're far from plas-tic.

Talk a-bout get-tin' blast-ed. I hate these blurred lines. I know you want it.

I know you want it. I know you want it. You're a good girl.

The way you grab me, must wan-na get nas-ty.

5

Go a - head, get at me. 3. What do they make dreams for

when you got them jeans on? What do we need steam for?

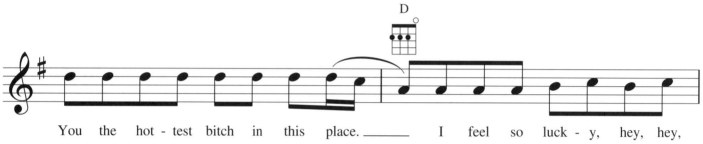

You the hot - test bitch in this place. _____ I feel so luck - y, hey, hey,

hey. You wan - na hug me, hey, hey, hey. What rhymes with hug me? Hey, hey,

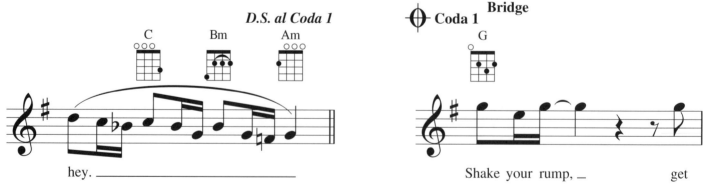

hey. _____ Shake your rump, _____ get

down. Get up, _____ ah. Do it like it

hurt, — like it hurt. — What? You don't like

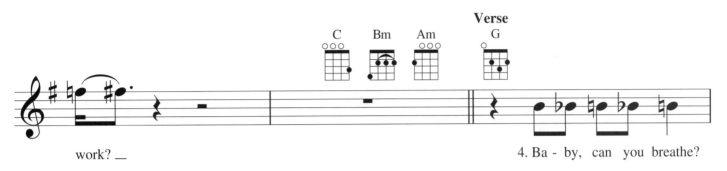

Verse

work? — 4. Ba - by, can you breathe?

I got this from Ja - mai - ca. It al - ways works for me, _____

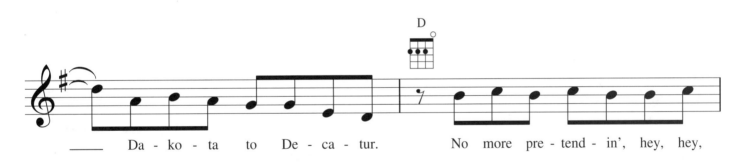

_____ Da - ko - ta to De - ca - tur. No more pre - tend - in', hey, hey,

hey, 'cause now you win - nin', hey, hey, hey. Here's our be - gin - nin', hey, hey,

D.S.S. al Coda 2   **Coda 2**

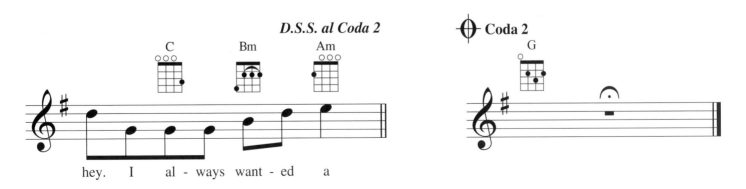

hey. I al - ways want - ed a

Cruise

Words and Music by Chase Rice, Tyler Hubbard, Brian Kelley, Joey Moi and Jesse Rice

First note

Intro
Moderately, in 2

Ba- by, you a song. You make me wan- na roll __ my win- dows down and

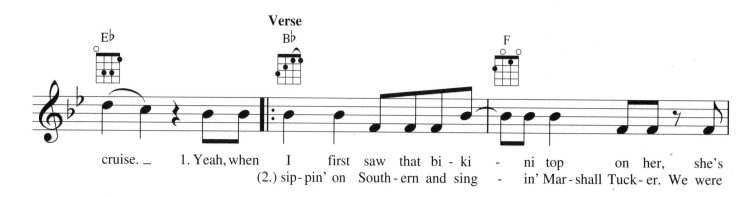

Verse

cruise. __ 1. Yeah, when I first saw that bi- ki - ni top on her, she's
(2.) sip- pin' on South- ern and sing - in' Mar- shall Tuck- er. We were

pop - pin' right out - ta the South __ Geor - gia wa - ter. Thought, "Oh, __
fall - in' in love in the sweet __ heart of sum - mer. She

___ good Lord!" __ She had them long, tanned legs. Could - n't
hopped right up __ in - to the cab of my truck and said,

2. Well, she was

When that ___

Bridge

___ sum - mer sun fell to his knees, ___ I ___ looked at her and she ___

___ looked at me and I turned on those K - C lights and drove ___

___ all night 'cause it felt so right. ___ Her and I, ___ man, we felt ___

Verse

___ so right. ___ 3. I put it in park and grabbed ___

Cups
(When I'm Gone)

from the Motion Picture Soundtrack PITCH PERFECT
Words and Music by A.P. Carter, Luisa Gerstein and Heloise Tunstall-Behrens

Counting Stars

Words and Music by Ryan Tedder

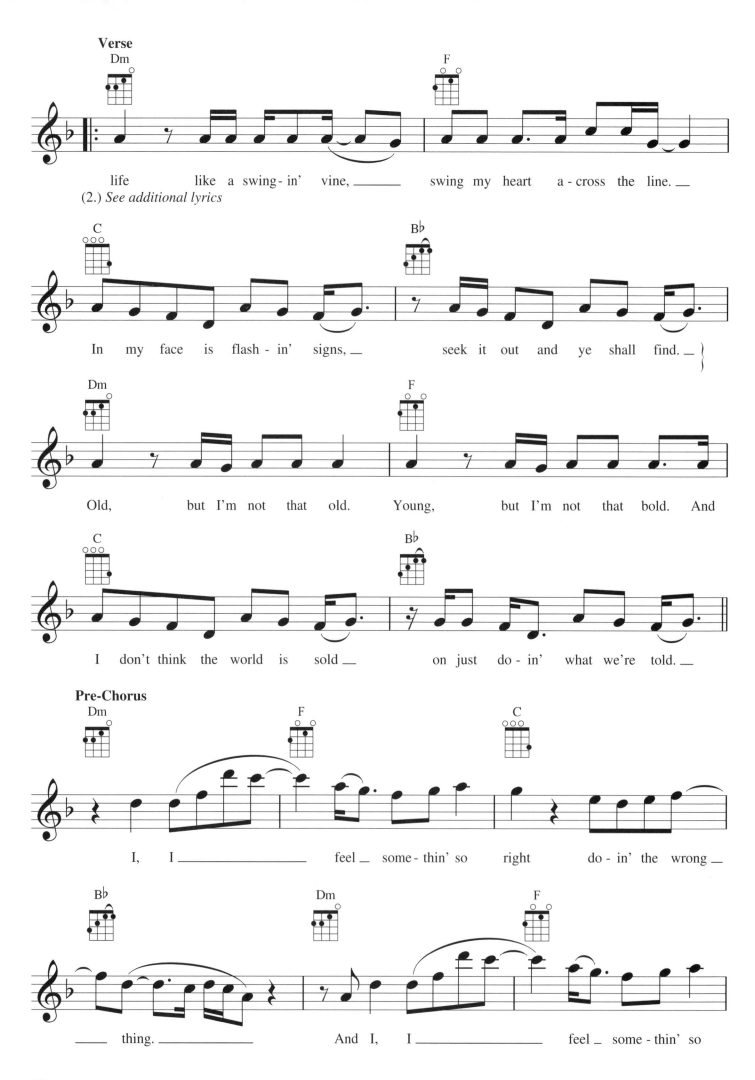

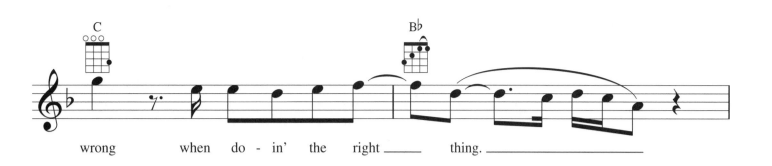

wrong   when do - in' the right &_____ thing. _____

I could - n't lie, could - n't   lie, could - n't lie. _____   Ev - 'ry - thing _ that
Ev - 'ry - thing _ that

kills   me   makes me   feel a - live.   Late - ly   I   been, _
drowns   me   makes me   wan - na fly.

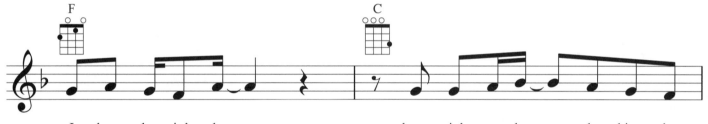

I been los - in' sleep _____   dream - in' a - bout _ the things that

we could be.   But, ba - by, I been, _   I been pray - in' hard. _

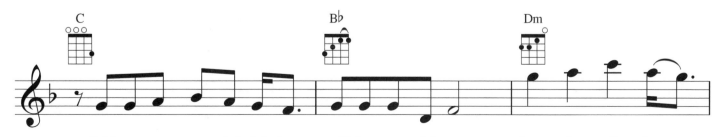

Said no more count - in' dol - lars, we'll be count - in' stars.   Late - ly   I   been, _

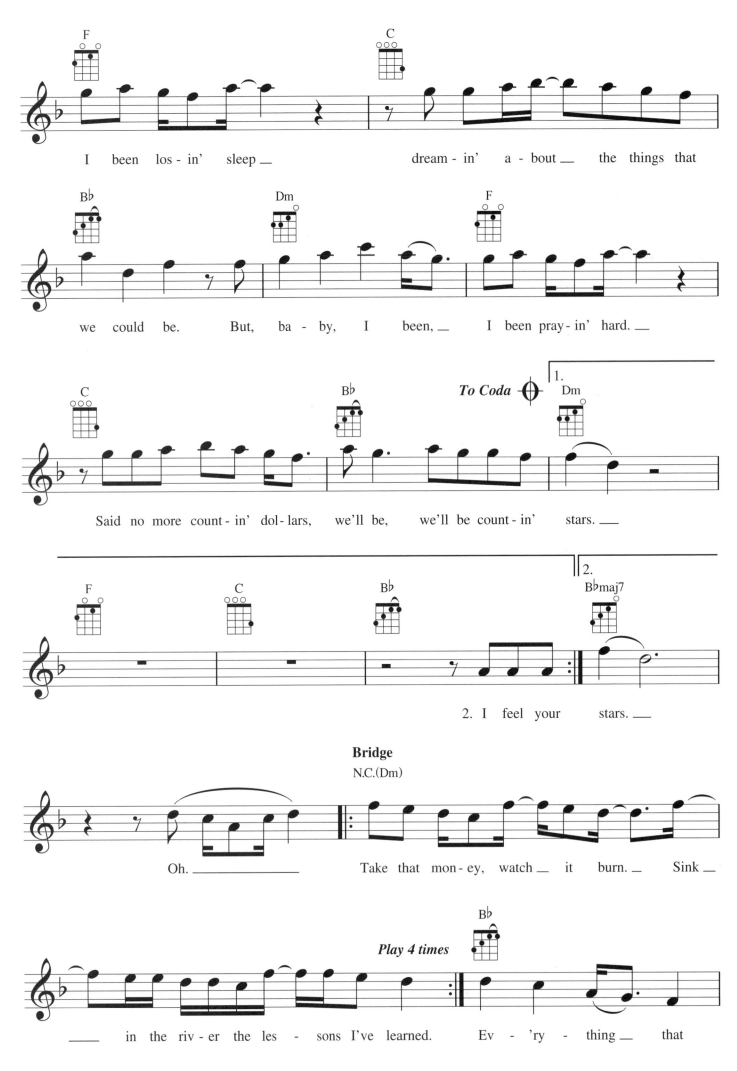

I been los - in' sleep __ dream - in' a - bout __ the things that

we could be. But, ba - by, I been, __ I been pray - in' hard. __

To Coda

Said no more count - in' dol - lars, we'll be, we'll be count - in' stars. __

2. I feel your stars. __

Bridge

N.C.(Dm)

Oh. _____ Take that mon - ey, watch __ it burn. __ Sink __

Play 4 times

____ in the riv - er the les - sons I've learned. Ev - 'ry - thing __ that

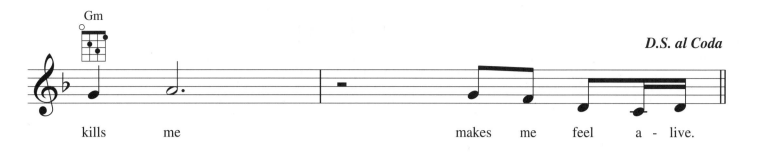

D.S. al Coda

kills me   makes me feel a - live.

⊕ Coda
Outro-Bridge

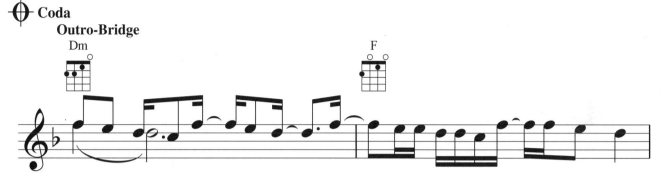

Take that mon - ey, watch _ it burn. _ Sink _ in the riv - er the les - sons I've learned.
stars. _____

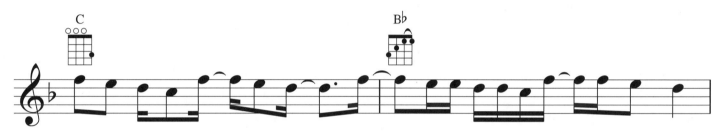

Take that mon - ey, watch _ it burn. _ Sink _ in the riv - er the les - sons I've learned.

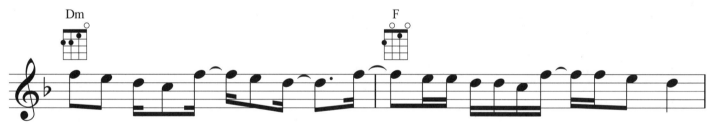

Take that mon - ey, watch _ it burn. _ Sink _ in the riv - er the les - sons I've learned.

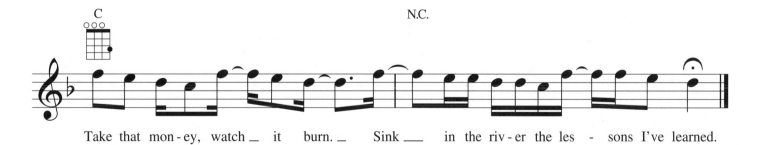

Take that mon - ey, watch _ it burn. _ Sink _ in the riv - er the les - sons I've learned.

Additional Lyrics

2. I feel your love, and I feel it burn
   Down this river, every turn.
   Hope is a four-letter word.
   Make that money, watch it burn.

Get Lucky

Words and Music by Thomas Bangalter, Guy Manuel Homem Christo,
Pharrell Williams and Nile Rodgers

Pre-Chorus

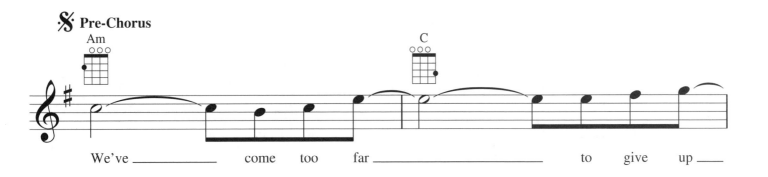

We've _____ come too far _____ to give up _____

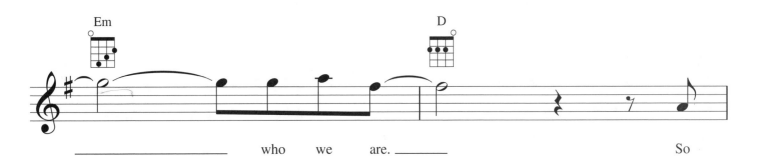

_____ who we are. _____ So

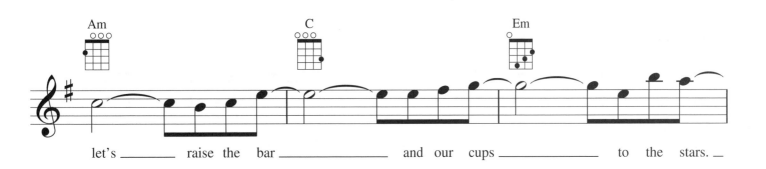

let's _____ raise the bar _____ and our cups _____ to the stars. _____

Chorus

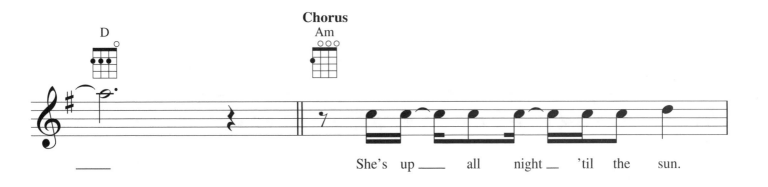

_____ She's up ____ all night ____ 'til the sun.

I'm up ____ all night ____ to get some. She's up ____ all night ____ for good fun.

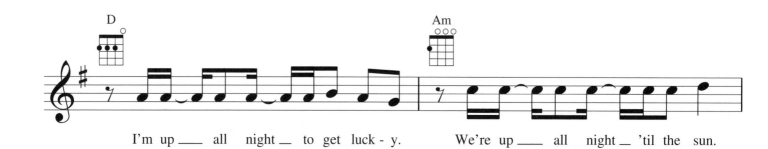

I'm up ____ all night ____ to get luck - y.   We're up ____ all night ____ 'til the sun.

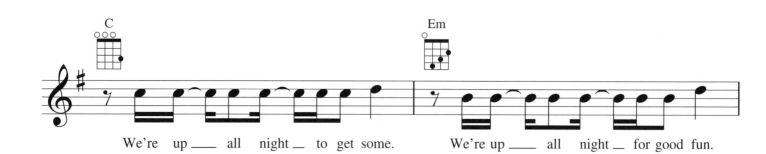

We're up ____ all night ____ to get some.   We're up ____ all night ____ for good fun.

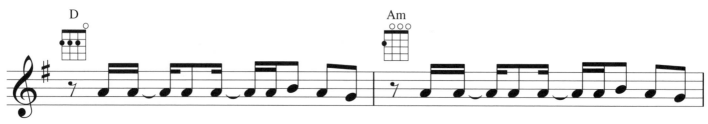

We're up ____ all night ____ to get luck - y.   We're up ____ all night ____ to get luck - y.

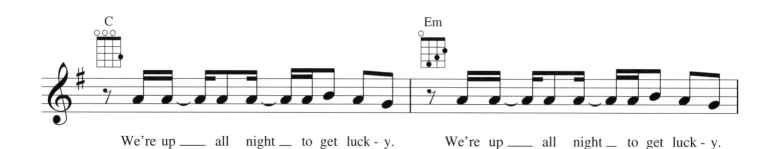

We're up ____ all night ____ to get luck - y.   We're up ____ all night ____ to get luck - y.

1.   2., 3.   *To Coda* ⊕

We're up ____ all night ____ to get luck - y.   We're up ____ all night ____ to get luck - y.

Bridge

We're up ___ all night ___ to get luck - y.   We're up ___ all night ___ to get luck - y.

2nd time, D.S. al Coda
(take 2nd ending)

We're up ___ all night ___ to get luck - y.   We're up ___ all night ___ to get luck - y.

⊕ Coda
Outro

We're up ___ all   night ___ to get   luck - y.

We're up ___ all night ___ to get luck - y.   We're up ___ all night ___ to get luck - y.

We're up ___ all   night ___ to get   luck - y.

Let Her Go

Words and Music by Michael David Rosenberg

Well, you on - ly need the light when it's burn - in' low.

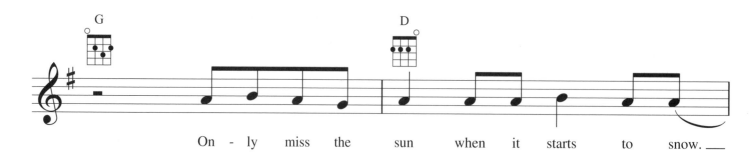

On - ly miss the sun when it starts to snow. __

__ On - ly know you love her when you let her go.

On - ly know _ you've been high when you're feel - in' low.

On - ly hate the road when you're miss - in' home. _ On - ly know you

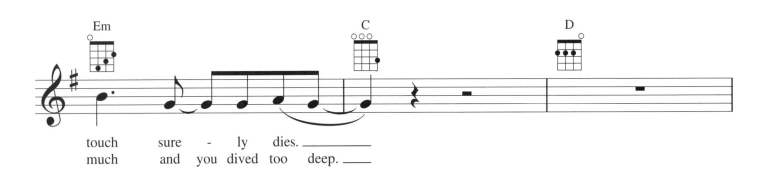

touch sure - ly dies. _____
much and you dived too deep. _____

𝄋 **Chorus**

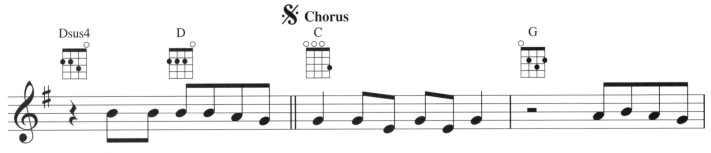

But } you on - ly need the light when it's burn - in' low. On - ly miss the
Well, }

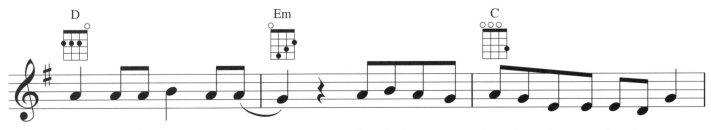

sun when it starts to snow. __ On - ly know you love her when you let her go.

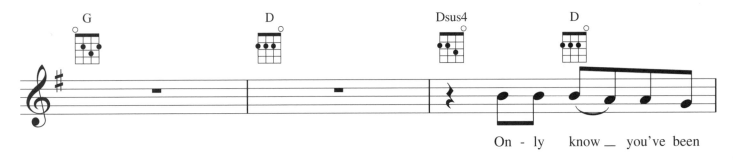

On - ly know __ you've been

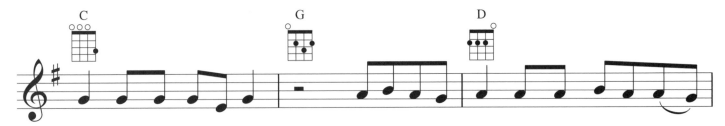

high when you're feel - in' low. On - ly hate the road when you're miss - in' home. _

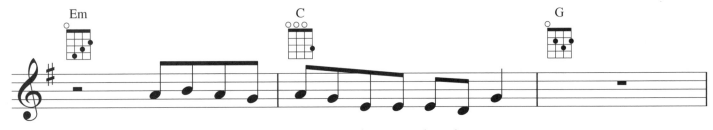

On - ly know you love her when you let her go.

Radioactive

Words and Music by Daniel Reynolds, Benjamin McKee, Daniel Sermon,
Alexander Grant and Josh Mosser

then check - ing out _____ on the pris - on bus.

This is it, _____ the A - poc - a - lypse. _____ Whoa, _____

𝄋 Chorus

I'm wak - ing up. I feel it in my bones, e -

nough to make my sys - tems blow. Wel - come to the new age,

to the new age. Wel - come to the new age, to the new age. _____

Whoa, _____ oh. Whoa, _____ I'm ra - di - o - ac - tive,

29

Just Give Me a Reason

Words and Music by Alecia Moore, Jeff Bhasker and Nate Ruess

Roar

Words and Music by Katy Perry, Lukasz Gottwald, Max Martin,
Bonnie McKee and Henry Walter

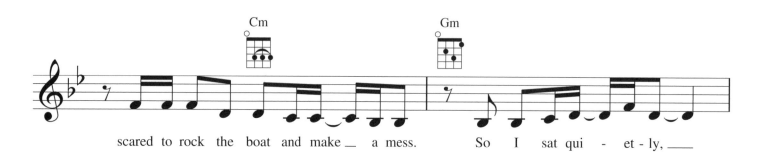

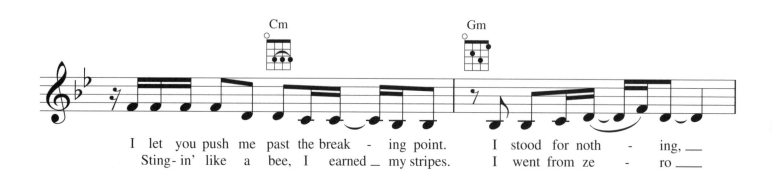

you're gon - na hear ___ me ___ roar. _____ Loud - er, loud -

er than a li - on 'cause I _____ am a cham - pion and

you're gon - na hear ___ me ___ roar, _____

oh, _____ oh. _____

1.

You're gon - na hear ___ me ___ roar. _____

2., 3.

You're gon - na hear ___ me ___ roar, _____

Safe and Sound

Words and Music by Ryan Takacs Merchant and Sebouh (Sebu) Simonian

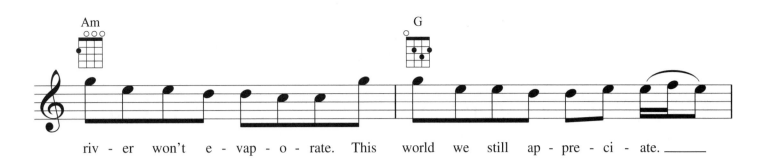

riv - er won't e - vap - o - rate. This world we still ap - pre - ci - ate. _____

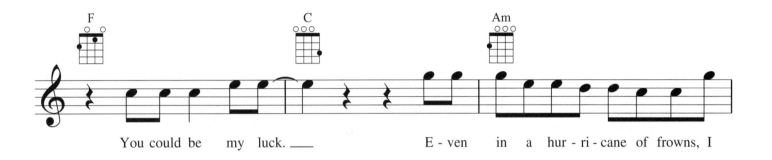

You could be my luck. ___ E - ven in a hur - ri - cane of frowns, I

Chorus

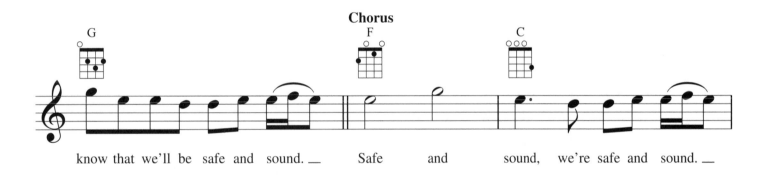

know that we'll be safe and sound. __ Safe and sound, we're safe and sound. __

Safe and sound, we're safe and sound. Hold your

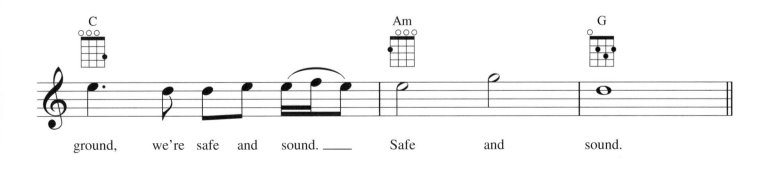

ground, we're safe and sound. _____ Safe and sound.

Bridge

I could show you love. ___ In a tid-al wave of mys-ter-y, you'll

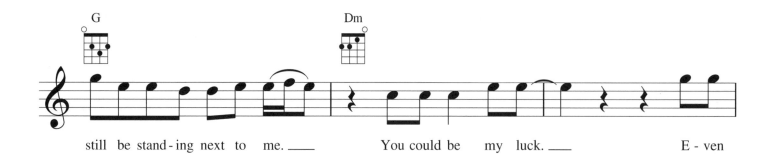

still be stand-ing next to me. ___ You could be my luck. ___ E-ven

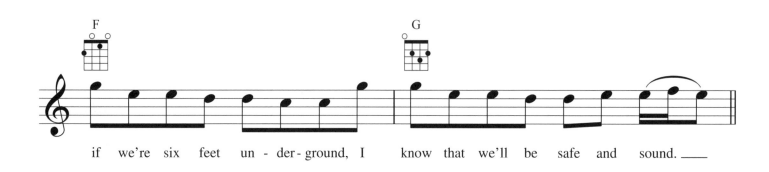

if we're six feet un-der-ground, I know that we'll be safe and sound. ___

Chorus

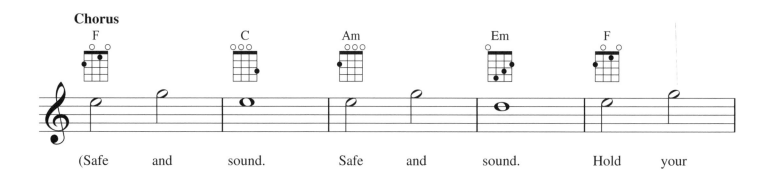

(Safe and sound. Safe and sound. Hold your

Outro

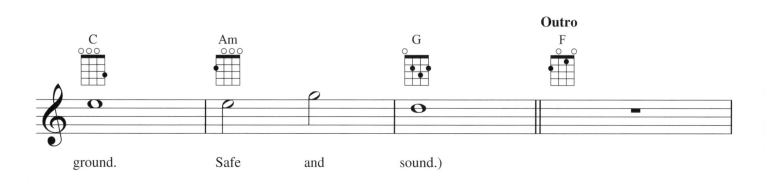

ground. Safe and sound.)

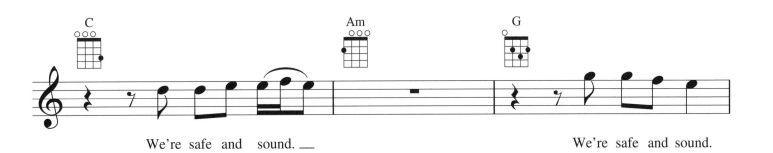

We're safe and sound. ___   We're safe and sound.

We're safe and sound. ___

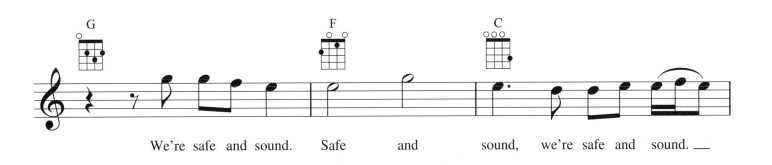

We're safe and sound.   Safe   and   sound,   we're safe and sound. ___

Safe   and   sound,   we're safe and sound.   Hold   your

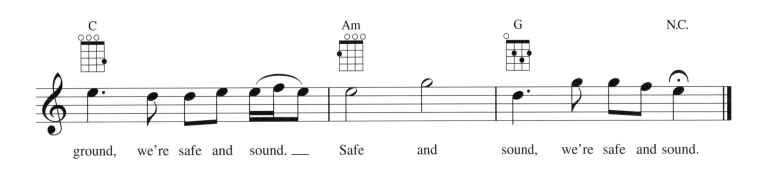

ground,   we're safe and sound. ___   Safe   and   sound,   we're safe and sound.

Say Something

Words and Music by Ian Axel, Chad Vaccarino and Mike Campbell

Say some-thing; I'm giv-ing up on you.

Verse

1. And I

am feel-ing so ___ small.

It was ___ o - ver my ___ head; I know

noth - ing at ___ all. ___ 2. And

Verse

I
(3.) I

will stum - ble and ___
will swal - low my ___

45

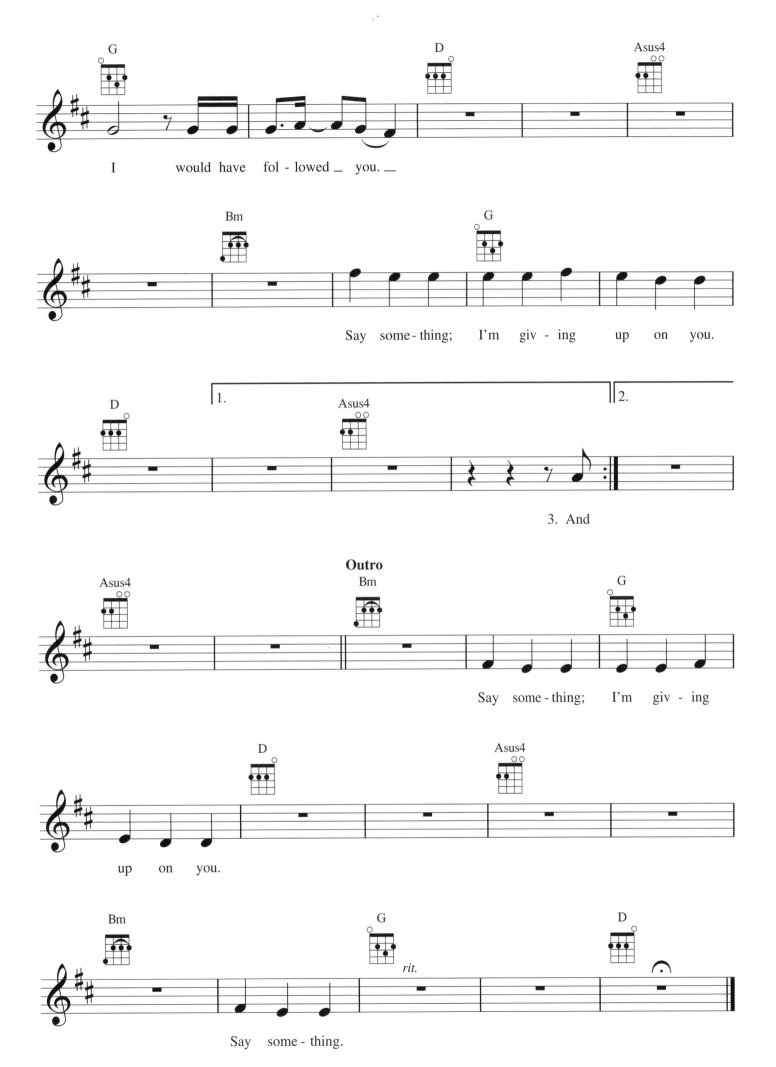

Wake Me Up!

Words and Music by Tim Bergling, Michael Einziger and Aloe Blacc

50

C G Am F C
- ver, when I'm wis - er and I'm old - er. All this
To Coda
Am F C G
time I was find - in' my - self and I / and I,
Am F C
did - n't know I was lost.
Verse
Am F C
2. I tried car - ry - ing the weight of the world,
Am F C
but I on - ly have two hands.
Am F C
Hope I get a chance to trav - el the world,

but I don't have ___ an - y plans. _____

Wish that I ___ could stay ___ for - ev - er this young. _____

Not a - fraid ___ to close ___ my eyes. _____

Life's a game _____ made ___ for ev - 'ry - one

and love is the prize. _____ So wake me

Coda

I did - n't know ___ I ___ was lost. _____

51

When I Was Your Man

Words and Music by Bruno Mars, Ari Levine, Philip Lawrence and Andrew Wyatt

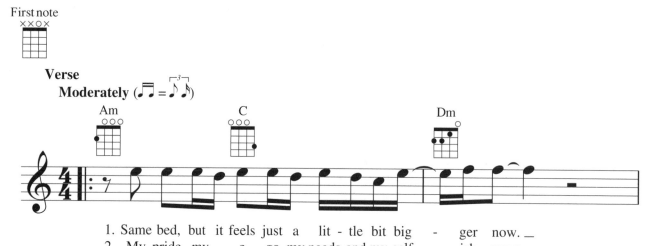

1. Same bed, but it feels just a lit - tle bit big - ger now. ___
2. My pride, my ___ e - go, my needs and my self - ish ways ___

Our song on the ra - di - o, but it don't sound ___ the same. ___
caused a good strong ___ wom - an like you to walk out ___ my life. ___

When our friends talk a - bout you, all it does is just tear ___ me down, ___
Now I ___ nev - er get to clean up the mess ___ I've ___ made, ___

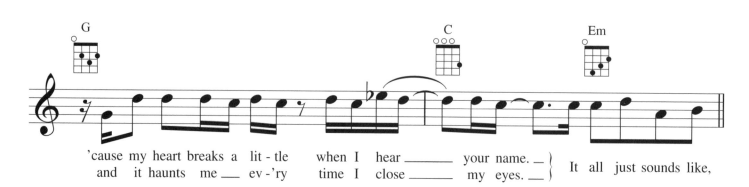

'cause my heart breaks a lit - tle when I hear ___ your name. ___ }
and it haunts me ___ ev - 'ry time I close ___ my eyes. ___ }

It all just sounds like,

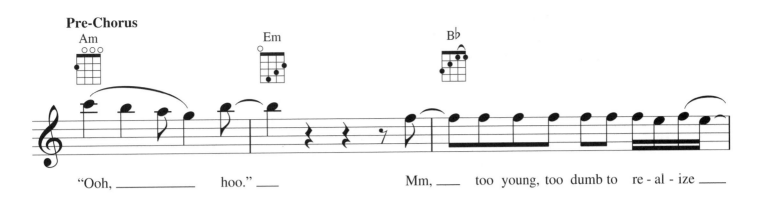

Pre-Chorus

"Ooh, _____ hoo." __ Mm, __ too young, too dumb to re - al - ize __

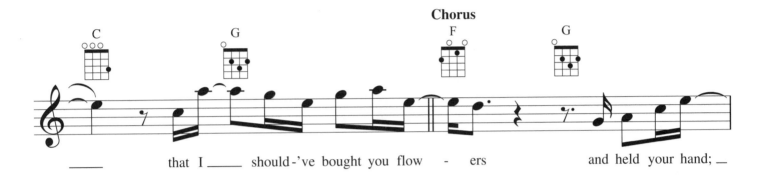

Chorus

____ that I __ should -'ve bought you flow - ers and held your hand; __

____ should -'ve gave you all my hours _____ when I had __ the

chance; take __ you to ev - 'ry par - ty, 'cause all __ you want - ed to do __ was dance. __

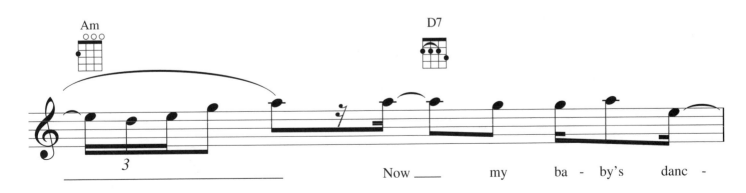

Now __ my ba - by's danc -

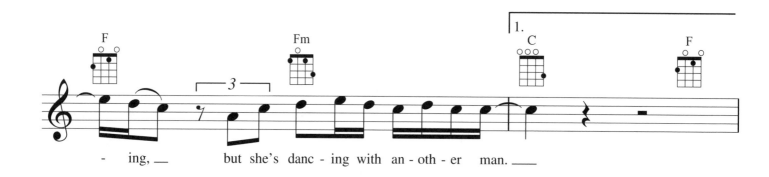

- ing, __ but she's danc - ing with an - oth - er man. __

__ Al - though it hurts, I'll be the __

first to say __ that I was wrong. __ Oh, I

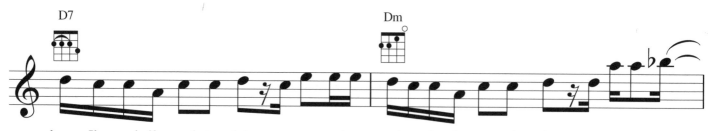

know I'm prob -'ly much too late to try and a - pol-o-gize for my mis-takes, but I just want __

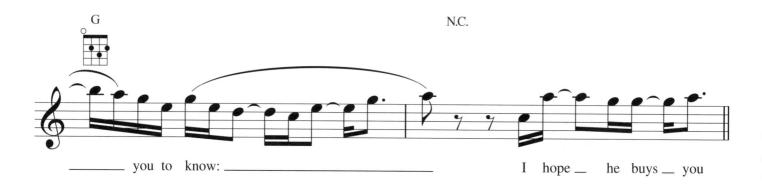

__ you to know: __ I hope __ he buys __ you

Chorus

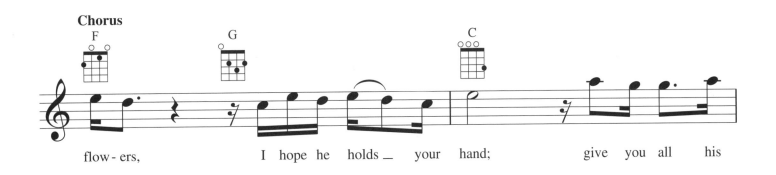

flow- ers,   I hope he holds __ your hand;   give you all his

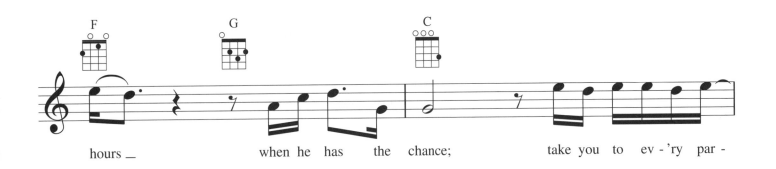

hours __   when he has the chance;   take you to ev -'ry par -

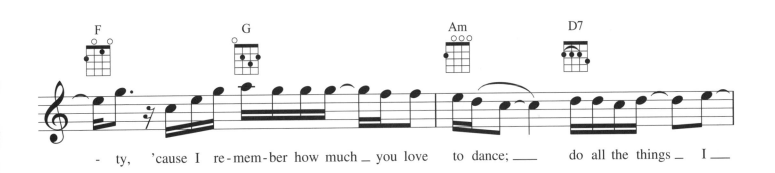

- ty, 'cause I re-mem-ber how much __ you love to dance; __ do all the things __ I __

__ should -'ve done __   when I was your man.   Do all the things I __

__ should -'ve done   when I was your man.

Wrecking Ball

**Words and Music by Stephan Richard Moccio, Maureen McDonald, Sacha Skarbek,
Lukasz Gottwald and Henry Walter**

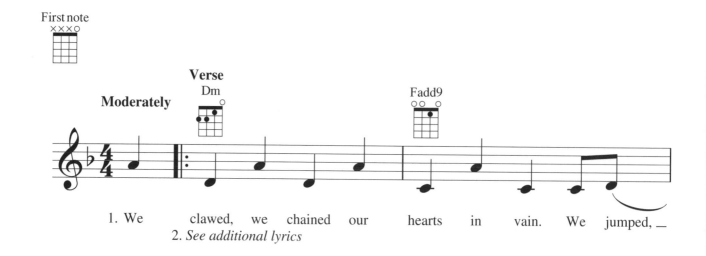

1. We clawed, we chained our hearts in vain. We jumped, __
2. *See additional lyrics*

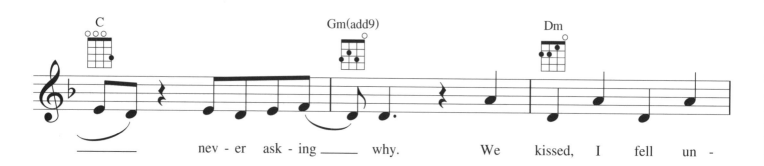

__ nev - er ask - ing __ why. We kissed, I fell un -

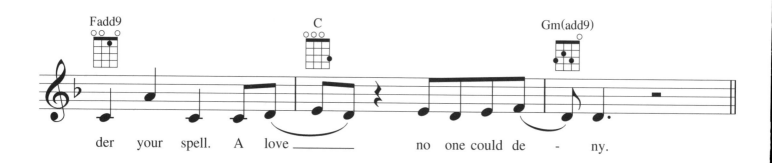

der your spell. A love __ no one could de - ny.

Don't you ev - er say I __ just walked a - way. I __ will al - ways want __

Additional Lyrics

2. I put you high up in the sky,
   And now, you're not coming down.
   It slowly turned; you let me burn,
   And now, we're ashes on the ground.

Royals

Words and Music by Ella Yelich-O'Connor and Joel Little

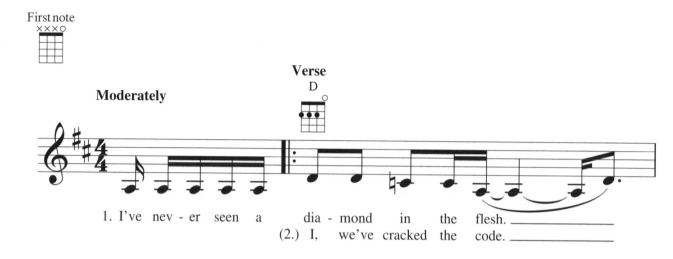

First note

Moderately

Verse
D

1. I've nev-er seen a dia-mond in the flesh. _____
(2.) I, we've cracked the code. _____

I cut my teeth on wed-ding rings ___ in the
We count our dol-lars on the train ___ to the

mov - ies. ___ And I'm not proud of my ad-dress. _____
par - ty. ___ And ev - 'ry - one who knows us knows _____

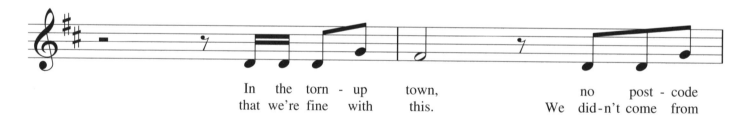

In the torn - up town, no post - code
that we're fine with this. We did-n't come from

Pre-Chorus
D

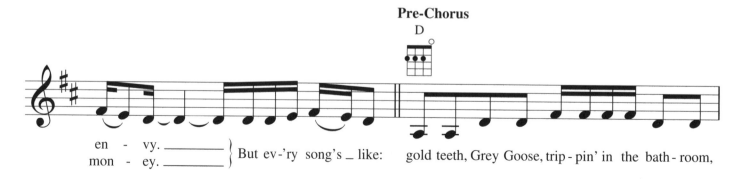

en - vy. _____ } But ev-'ry song's _ like: gold teeth, Grey Goose, trip - pin' in the bath - room,
mon - ey. _____

blood stains, ball gowns, trash-in' the ho-tel room. We don't care, __ we're driv-in'

Cad-il-lacs in our dreams. _ But ev-'ry-bod-y's like: Cris-tal, May-bach, dia-monds on your time-piece,

jet planes, is-lands, ti-gers on a gold leash. We don't care, __ we aren't

𝄋 **Chorus**

caught up in your love af-fair. __ And we'll nev-er be roy-als, (roy-als.)

It don't run in our _ blood. _ That kind of luxe just ain't _ for us. __ We crave a

dif-f'rent kind _ of buzz. _ Let me be _ your rul-er, (rul-er.)

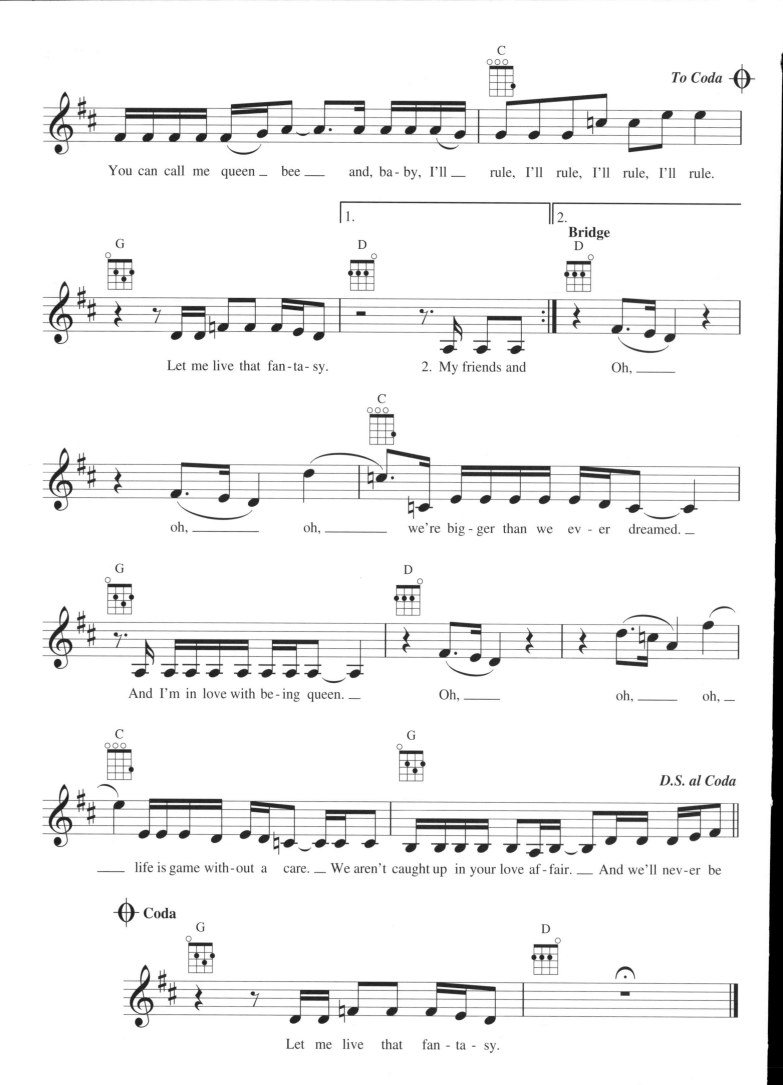

HAL·LEONARD UKULELE PLAY-ALONG

Now you can play your favorite songs on your uke with great-sounding backing tracks to help you sound like a bona fide pro! This series includes the Amazing Slow Downer, so you can adjust the tempo without changing the pitch.

1. POP HITS
00701451 Book/CD Pack..........................$14.99

2. UKE CLASSICS
00701452 Book/CD Pack..........................$12.99

3. HAWAIIAN FAVORITES
00701453 Book/CD Pack..........................$12.99

4. CHILDREN'S SONGS
00701454 Book/CD Pack..........................$12.99

5. CHRISTMAS SONGS
00701696 Book/CD Pack..........................$12.99

6. LENNON & MCCARTNEY
00701723 Book/CD Pack..........................$12.99

7. DISNEY FAVORITES
00701724 Book/CD Pack..........................$12.99

8. CHART HITS
00701745 Book/CD Pack..........................$14.99

9. THE SOUND OF MUSIC
00701784 Book/CD Pack..........................$12.99

10. MOTOWN
00701964 Book/CD Pack..........................$12.99

11. CHRISTMAS STRUMMING
00702458 Book/CD Pack..........................$12.99

12. BLUEGRASS FAVORITES
00702584 Book/CD Pack..........................$12.99

13. UKULELE SONGS
00702599 Book/CD Pack..........................$12.99

14. JOHNNY CASH
00702615 Book/CD Pack..........................$14.99

15. COUNTRY CLASSICS
00702834 Book/CD Pack..........................$12.99

16. STANDARDS
00702835 Book/CD Pack..........................$12.99

17. POP STANDARDS
00702836 Book/CD Pack..........................$12.99

18. IRISH SONGS
00703086 Book/CD Pack..........................$12.99

19. BLUES STANDARDS
00703087 Book/CD Pack..........................$12.99

20. FOLK POP ROCK
00703088 Book/CD Pack..........................$12.99

21. HAWAIIAN CLASSICS
00703097 Book/CD Pack..........................$12.99

22. ISLAND SONGS
00703098 Book/CD Pack..........................$12.99

23. TAYLOR SWIFT
00704106 Book/CD Pack..........................$14.99

24. WINTER WONDERLAND
00101871 Book/CD Pack..........................$12.99

25. GREEN DAY
00110398 Book/CD Pack..........................$14.99

26. BOB MARLEY
00110399 Book/CD Pack..........................$14.99

27. TIN PAN ALLEY
00116358 Book/CD Pack..........................$12.99

HAL·LEONARD® CORPORATION

7777 W. BLUEMOUND RD. P.O. BOX 13819 MILWAUKEE, WI 53213

www.halleonard.com

Prices, contents, and availability subject to change without notice.

0314

Ride the Ukulele Wave!

The Beach Boys for Ukulele

This folio features 20 favorites, including: Barbara Ann • Be True to Your School • California Girls • Fun, Fun, Fun • God Only Knows • Good Vibrations • Help Me Rhonda • I Get Around • In My Room • Kokomo • Little Deuce Coupe • Sloop John B • Surfin' U.S.A. • Wouldn't It Be Nice • and more!

00701726 . . . . $14.99

The Beatles for Ukulele

Ukulele players can strum, sing and pick along with 20 Beatles classics! Includes: All You Need Is Love • Eight Days a Week • Good Day Sunshine • Here, There and Everywhere • Let It Be • Love Me Do • Penny Lane • Yesterday • and more.

00700154 . . . . $16.99

The Daily Ukulele

compiled and arranged by Liz and Jim Beloff

Strum a different song everyday with easy arrangements of 365 of your favorite songs in one big songbook! Includes favorites by the Beatles, Beach Boys, and Bob Dylan, folk songs, pop songs, kids' songs, Christmas carols, and Broadway and Hollywood tunes, all with a spiral binding for ease of use.

00240356 . . . . $34.99

The Daily Ukulele – Leap Year Edition

366 More Songs for Better Living

compiled and arranged by Liz and Jim Beloff

An amazing second volume with 366 MORE songs for you to master each day of a leap year! Includes: Ain't No Sunshine • Calendar Girl • I Got You Babe • Lean on Me • Moondance • and many, many more.

00240681 . . . . $34.99

Disney Songs for Ukulele

20 great Disney classics arranged for all uke players, including: Beauty and the Beast • Bibbidi-Bobbidi-Boo (The Magic Song) • Can You Feel the Love Tonight • Chim Chim Cher-ee • Heigh-Ho • It's a Small World • Some Day My Prince Will Come • We're All in This Together • When You Wish upon a Star • and more.

00701708 . . . . $12.99

Folk Songs for Ukulele

A great collection to take along to the campfire! 60 folk songs, including: Amazing Grace • Buffalo Gals • Camptown Races • For He's a Jolly Good Fellow • Good Night Ladies • Home on the Range • I've Been Working on the Railroad • Kumbaya • My Bonnie Lies over the Ocean • On Top of Old Smoky • Scarborough Fair • Swing Low, Sweet Chariot • Take Me Out to the Ball Game • Yankee Doodle • and more.

00696068 . . . . $12.99

Glee

Music from the Fox Television Show for Ukulele

20 favorites for Gleeks to strum and sing, including: Bad Romance • Beautiful • Defying Gravity • Don't Stop Believin' • No Air • Proud Mary • Rehab • True Colors • and more.

00701722 . . . . $14.99

Hawaiian Songs for Ukulele

Over thirty songs from the state that made the ukulele famous, including: Beyond the Rainbow • Hanalei Moon • Ka-lu-a • Lovely Hula Girl • Mele Kalikimaka • One More Aloha • Sea Breeze • Tiny Bubbles • Waikiki • and more.

00696065 . . . . $9.99

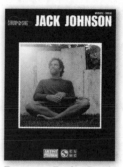

Jack Johnson – Strum & Sing

Cherry Lane Music

Strum along with 41 Jack Johnson songs using this top-notch collection of chords and lyrics just for the uke! Includes: Better Together • Bubble Toes • Cocoon • Do You Remember • Flake • Fortunate Fool • Good People • Holes to Heaven • Taylor • Tomorrow Morning • and more.

02501702 . . . . $12.99

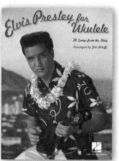

Elvis Presley for Ukulele

arr. Jim Beloff

20 classic hits from The King: All Shook Up • Blue Hawaii • Blue Suede Shoes • Can't Help Falling in Love • Don't • Heartbreak Hotel • Hound Dog • Jailhouse Rock • Love Me • Love Me Tender • Return to Sender • Suspicious Minds • Teddy Bear • and more.

00701004 . . . . $14.99

Jake Shimabukuro – Peace Love Ukulele

Deemed "the Hendrix of the ukulele," Hawaii native Jake Shimabukuro is a uke virtuoso. Our songbook features note-for-note transcriptions with ukulele tablature of Jake's masterful playing on all the CD tracks: Bohemian Rhapsody • Boy Meets Girl • Bring Your Adz • Hallelujah • Pianoforte 2010 • Variation on a Dance 2010 • and more, plus two bonus selections!

00702516 . . . . $19.99

Worship Songs for Ukulele

25 worship songs: Amazing Grace (My Chains are Gone) • Blessed Be Your Name • Enough • God of Wonders • Holy Is the Lord • How Great Is Our God • In Christ Alone • Love the Lord • Mighty to Save • Sing to the King • Step by Step • We Fall Down • and more.

00702546 . . . . $12.99

HAL•LEONARD® CORPORATION

7777 W. BLUEMOUND RD. P.O. BOX 13819 MILWAUKEE, WI 53213

0314